A GUIDE TO

HISTORIC HAMILTON

This book was made possible in part by funding
from the Montana Cultural Trust, Daly Mansion Preservation
Trust, Soroptimists International of Hamilton, Ravalli County
Museum, Bitterroot Valley Chamber of Commerce, Citizens State
Bank, Hamilton Business Organization, Ravalli County Bank, and
the Downtown Hamilton Business Improvement District.

Montana Mainstreets

VOLUME FOUR

A GUIDE TO
HISTORIC HAMILTON

by CHERE JIUSTO

WITH A PREFACE BY
Mark F. Baumler, State Historic Preservation
Officer of Montana

AND AN AFTERWORD BY
Russ Lawrence

MONTANA
HISTORICAL
SOCIETY
PRESS

COVER IMAGE Hamilton, Labor Day parade on Main Street,
circa 1910, MHS Photo Archives

COVER DESIGN Kathryn Fehlig
BOOK DESIGN Arrow Graphics, Missoula
TYPESET IN Stempel Schneidler

The photographs in this book are from the following sources: Bitter Root Valley
Historical Society, Hamilton (BVHS); Glenbow Museum, Calgary (Glenbow);
Maureen and Mike Mansfield Library, University of Montana, Missoula (UM);
Montana Historical Society Library, Helena (MHS Library); Montana
Historical Society Photo Archives, Helena (MHS Photo Archives); and
Montana Historical Society State Historic Preservation Office (SHPO).
Line art was drawn by Ken Sievert, Great Falls.

PRINTED BY Advanced Litho Printing, Great Falls

MONTANA
CULTURAL
TRUST
Partial funding for this project was provided by Montana's Cultural Trust.

00 01 02 03 04 05 06 07 08   10 9 8 7 6 5 4 3 2 1

LIBRARY OF CONGRESS CATALOGING-IN-PUBLICATION DATA

Juisto, Chere.
    A guide to historic Hamilton / by Chere Jiusto; with a foreword by Mark
Baumler; and an afterword by Russ Lawrence.
        p.   cm. — (Montana mainstreets ; v. 4)
    Includes bibliographical references and index.
    ISBN 0-917298-67-5 (pbk. : alk. paper)
    1. Historic sites—Montana—Hamilton—Guidebooks. 2. Hamilton (Mont.)—
Tours. 3. Hamilton (Mont.)—History. I. Montana Historical Society. II. Series.
F739.H34 G85   2000
978.6'89—dc21   00-042110

Contents

Preface

MONTANA MAINSTREETS invites you to take a new look at a number of Montana towns. Based in large part on State Historic Preservation Office files, this series explores Montana's past using standing historic buildings—businesses, institutions, and homes—to illustrate the stories of some of the state's most intriguing communities. The information in these volumes derives from the Preservation Office's effort to inventory historic places statewide and identify those eligible for listing in the National Register of Historic Places. This work began in the 1970s and continues today.

Some readers may be surprised to learn that historic buildings, perhaps located in their own town, are or could be listed in the National Register. Isn't such designation reserved for architectural masterpieces, the birthplaces of American heroes, the oldest, the biggest, and the best in the nation? While such places—including some in Montana—often qualify for recognition, they alone do not constitute the National Register of Historic Places. The National Register is designed to recognize properties of importance to local communities, not just great national landmarks. Thus, it includes buildings associated with local and state events and personages; homes representative of architectural styles and period craftsmanship; and even archaeological sites that offer glimpses of places and people no longer visible. The goal of community historic surveys is less about identifying a "top ten" and more about recognizing how a variety of places, buildings, streets, and neighborhoods combine to reflect a town's history and the sense of place of its residents.

In these volumes you will read about communities where history is not only past but also very much present. These are not ghost towns frozen in time. The historic built environment is neither obsolete nor abandoned. In these communities, historic homes and commercial quarters continue to contribute today—economically, socially, politically, and aesthetically—to their town's livelihood and purpose. They are testimonies that historic preservation makes sense.

With few exceptions, only historic buildings (those at least fifty years old) are listed in the National Register, and of these only some can be highlighted in these slim volumes. Not every historic or architecturally significant structure is illustrated, nor every story told. Therefore, in addition to providing information on specific properties, these guides are designed to educate readers about local historical trends, styles, and developments to assist them in better understanding other buildings in the featured communities and across Montana. The real value is where these books can take you from here.

Among my archaeologist friends there is a saying: Forward into the past! I trust you will heed this invitation in your journey down Montana's historical mainstreets.

MARK F. BAUMLER
State Historic Preservation
Officer of Montana

How to Use This Guide

+≈≈+

THIS GUIDEBOOK has a twofold purpose. First, to draw you in, to discover the historical mosaic that is Hamilton, Montana. And second, to send you out, to tour and explore for yourself the historical places that lie within the borders of this century-old community.

The first half of the book spins out four distinct stories all acted upon the same stage. A story of ancient origins and the native peoples who made the Bitterroot Valley their ancestral home. A tale of timber and settlement, when copper baron Marcus Daly very purposely planted the seeds of a company town of his own design and making. The drama of the apple boom years, when the rosy blush of McIntosh Reds lured thousands of newcomers deep into this remote valley. And the saga of the tick fever battle, when white-coated pioneers pitted their lives against a raging disease in search of a cure.

The second half introduces you to the town itself. Here you will find information on a very fine, well-tended collection of stylish historic homes and business blocks. The range of building styles and quality of craftsmanship sets this small town apart from many others.

In 1987 the Hamilton Historic Resource Survey was launched to survey and make a record of all the historical buildings within the early townsite. Under the guidance of project director

Kirk Michels and volunteer leader Ada Powell, Hamilton created one of the most thorough community historical surveys completed in Montana. The information in this book is drawn from that work and from the sources listed on pages 71–72. As author, I am indebted to all of those writers whose research I consulted to create this guide.

The town of Hamilton has a long and proud history, which has been faithfully kept by many members of the community, and over the years stories of the early days have been passed from one generation to the next. One person who has spent much of her life listening to those stories and recording the knowledge so we all may remember is Ada Powell. This guide is dedicated to her.

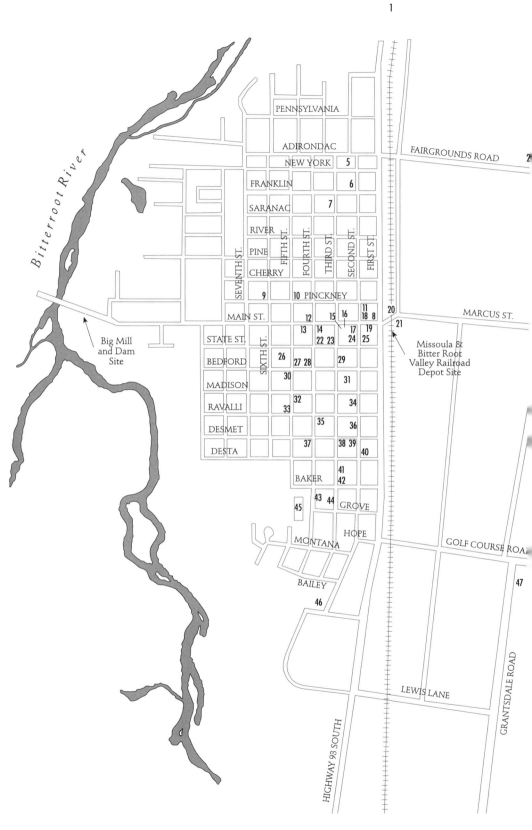

HAMILTON
Historic Sites

(year of construction in parentheses)

1. Montana-Utah Sugar Co. Smokestack, Highway 93 (1917)
2. Ravalli County Fairgrounds, Fairgrounds Rd. (1895)
3. Daly Mansion, 251 Eastside Highway (1910)
4. Tammany's Castle, Tammany Loop (1895)
5. Martha Allison-Reinkeh House, 207 Adirondac Ave. (ca. 1880)
6. Frank H. Drinkenberg House, 701 N. Second St. (1895)
7. Sherman Gill House, 605 N. Third St. (1907)
8. Bozeman Cannery, 315 N. First St. (1923)
9. Methodist Episcopal Church North, 207 N. Sixth St. (1896)
10. Other C. Wamsley House, 200 N. Fifth St. (1909)
11. Roxy Theater, 120–140 N. Second St. (1935)
12. Ravalli County Creamery, 404 W. Main St. (1933, 1946)
13. False-front Art City Building, 407 W. Main St. (1895)
14. Telephone Exchange Building, 339–345 W. Main St. (1936)
15. Ravalli County Bank, 225 W. Main St. (1895)
16. McGrath Block, 215–217 W. Main St. (1910)
17. Bower Building, 201–209 W. Main St. (1936) (original site of Anaconda Co. Store)
18. Ford's Clothing, 136 W. Main St. (1947)
19. Daly Block, 127 W. Main St. (1908–9)
20. Hamilton Warehouse Zone, Highway 93 (1895)
21. Bitter Root Development Company Warehouse, head of Main St. (ca. 1895)
22. Ravalli Public Library, 312 State St. (1916)
23. Hamilton City Hall and Fire House, 119 S. Third St. (1906)
24. First National Bank, 163–167 S. Second St. (1910)
25. Bitter Root Stock Farm Office, 166–170 S. Second St. (1909)
26. Hamilton High School, 209 S. Fifth St. (1930)
27. W. W. McCrackin House, 224 S. Fifth St. (1892)
28. Marcus Daly Memorial Hospital, 211 S. Fourth St. (1931)
29. Bibler Apartments, 212 S. Third St. (ca. 1930)
30. Hamilton Presbyterian Church, 319 S. Fifth St. (1893)
31. Ravalli County Courthouse, 205 Bedford St. (1900)
32. C. M. Crutchfield House, 402 S. Fifth St. (1895)
33. St. Francis Catholic Church, 417 S. Fifth St. (1896)
34. Bitter Root Development Office, 415 S. Second St. (1890)
35. Anaconda Company Workers' Cottages, 500 block S. Fourth St. (1895–1908)
36. Henry Grover House, 509 S. Second St. (ca. 1909)
37. Frank Meinhart House, 601 S. Fourth St. (1901)
38. St. Paul's Episcopal Church, 600 S. Third St. (1893)
39. First Christian Church, 601 S. Second St. (1895)
40. A. H. Downing House, 610 S. Second St. (1910)
41. Dr. Robert Getty House, 708 S. Third St. (ca. 1912)
42. Dr. George B. Taylor House, 710 S. Third St. (1935)
43. Pine Apartments, 804 S. Fourth St. (ca. 1938)
44. Charles Hoffman House, 807 S. Third St. (ca. 1914)
45. Rocky Mountain Laboratory, 903 S. Fourth St. (1928)
46. Elliot House, behind 1211 S. Second St. (1870s)
47. Doran Farm, 278 Grantsdale Rd. (1870s)

Salish winter camp in the Bitterroot Valley, ca. 1890
NA 1443-19, Peeso Collection, Glenbow

Historic Overview

OF BITTERROOTS AND RED WILLOWS

The Salish and Pend d'Oreille Indians tell of living here since the beginnings of human time; the valley Spe'tlemen is the heart of their ancestral homeland. Through this broad, fertile Bitterroot Valley flows the river called In-schu-te-sche, the River of Red Willows. Warmed by winds born over the Pacific Ocean, the valley teems with huckleberries, herons, lupine, deer, and bears. Long ago, Salish elders recount, a single Salish nation inhabited what is now western Montana; over time they formed distinctive tribes known now as the Salish and Pend d'Oreille, as well as the Couer d'Alene, Spokane, Colville, and Okinagan. For thousands of years, Salish people followed a way of life in this mountainous country attuned to the seasons and the land—hunting buffalo and other game, catching fish, collecting plant foods and medicines, trading between tribes and bands.

White Europeans came late to this western country. The first recorded encounter here occurred in September 1805, when the Lewis and Clark Expedition traveled through the Bitterroot Valley en route to "the great waters where the sun set." Just a boy at the time, Many Horses, or Chief Victor, later recounted how the "pale faced chiefs looked strange" to the Salish but were welcomed at their encampment in the Sula Basin. The Salish took them in, fed them, and "gave them fresh good horses" in exchange for their tired ones. These "ellegant" horses carried the explorers toward the distant shore of the Pacific along the ancient and rugged Lolo Trail.

Almost twenty years later, a North West Company fur trapping expedition led by Alexander Ross visited the Bitterroot Valley, and other Euramericans soon followed. Peter Skene Ogden, Jedediah Smith, and Jim Bridger, mountain men whose names are etched deeply into the tablets of the American West, were among those who opened the gateway of the Bitterroot and set a course toward eventual displacement of the Indian people who for so long had called this valley home.

The fur trade brought to the valley French Canadian fur traders and Iroquois trappers, who talked of Christianity and black-robed priests. Hoping to learn more about this religion, the Salish and Nez Perce sent four delegations to St. Louis during the 1830s, in search of a Black Robe to teach them. The last party secured Father Pierre-Jean DeSmet, a Belgian Jesuit priest, who journeyed to the 1840 trading rendezvous at Green River. That July he introduced a gathering of Salish, Nez Perce, and Shoshone to Christianity, and in "a spectacle truly moving for the heart of a missionary," he performed mass at the Deer Lodge Mound (at present-day Warm Springs, Montana).

Father DeSmet returned in 1841 with a party of missionaries, following the Salish to the heartland of their ancestral territory. Where Burnt Fork Creek flows into the Bitterroot River, the Black Robes christened it all—the mission, the river and the red mountain that towered over the valley—"St. Mary's."

By 1846 the relationship soured, particularly after the missionaries made overtures to the Salish's long-standing enemies,

Built by Father Anthony Ravalli, the second St. Mary's Mission still stands. It is one of the oldest buildings in the state. MHS Photo Archives

the Blackfeet. The mission was disbanded in 1850 and the property sold to Major John Owen for $250. Where the missionaries had failed, Owen opened a bustling trading post and befriended many Indian people. Fort Owen became an outpost of settlement, and John Owen became an Indian agent and important intermediary between the tribes and the white world moving in from the east.

Shortly thereafter Governor Isaac I. Stevens, of the newly created Washington Territory, traversed the area following orders to survey a rail route to the Pacific and clear the way for white settlement. At Council Grove (now on the edge of Missoula), in an ancient pine forest, the Salish were asked to abandon their Bitterroot Valley. The negotiations were confused by language barriers. The Salish resisted but finally agreed to move after the president of the United States ordered a

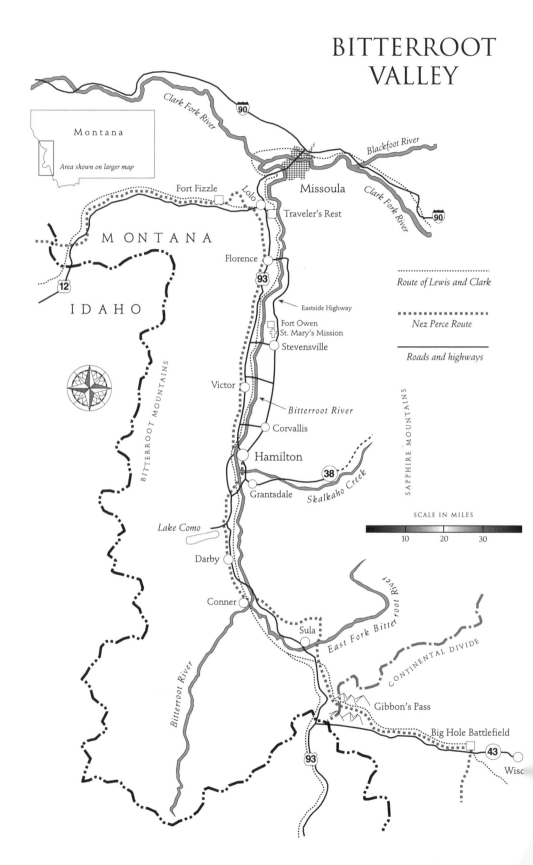

BITTERROOT VALLEY

Montana

Area shown on larger map

Clark Fork River

90

Blackfoot River

Clark Fork River

Missoula

90

Fort Fizzle

Lolo

Traveler's Rest

MONTANA

IDAHO

12

Florence

93

Eastside Highway

Fort Owen
St. Mary's Mission

Stevensville

BITTERROOT MOUNTAINS

Victor

Bitterroot River

Corvallis

Hamilton

38

SAPPHIRE MOUNTAINS

Grantsdale

Skalkaho Creek

Lake Como

Darby

Conner

Sula

East Fork Bitterroot River

CONTINENTAL DIVIDE

Bitterroot River

Gibbon's Pass

Big Hole Battlefield

93

43

Wisc

.... Route of Lewis and Clark

▪▪▪▪▪▪ Nez Perce Route

—— Roads and highways

SCALE IN MILES

10   20   30

survey and determined that the harsher Jocko Valley to the north better suited their needs. Until that decision was rendered, the Bitterroot remained closed to white settlers. But retired trappers, errant soldiers, and hopeful farmers, undaunted by the express illegality of claiming land in Indian territory, had other ideas. During the 1850s and 1860s, the Bitterroot Valley gave rise to a growing cultural mosaic of white farmers and tradesmen, mixed-blood traders and trappers, Indian wives, and many children. The sounds of cabin building, sodbusting, and prospect digging increasingly interrupted the dewy quiet of the Bitterroot.

"The impression in Circulation abroad is that this Entire Country is thrown open for Settlement under the treaty of 1855. White settlers are coming in & others are daily Expected . . . The Indians have Serious objections," wrote agent Owen in October 1859. But the pace of white settlement only quickened following 1860s gold strikes, passage of the 1862 Homestead Act, and, in 1864, the creation of Montana Territory. Settlement fanned out around Fort Owen (where St. Mary's mission was reopened) and began moving deeper into the Bitterroot.

In 1870 Chief Victor died, and the following year President Ulysses S. Grant ordered the Salish to move to the Jocko Valley reservation. To hasten their removal Grant dispatched then-congressman James A. Garfield who convinced Arlee and Ninepipes to move their bands north. Despite threats of bloodshed, Victor's son, Claw of the Grizzly Bear, or Chief Charlot, refused to submit to the removal; in the end his mark was forged onto the "Garfield agreement."

Garfield's diaries noted that John Owen had become "a bankrupt and a sot . . . Since the death of his Indian wife he has rapidly run down and is now quite a wreck." Owen's fort was auctioned to the highest bidder at the end of 1871, and Owen himself was committed to an asylum in Helena and in later years deported out of the territory to Philadelphia.

Chief Charlot and his band clung to the hope that they might stay in their ancestral homeland, but white settlers moving into the valley had little interest in sharing it. They clamored for more military protection against the Indians, and in 1877 the government established Fort Missoula near the confluence of the Bitterroot and the Clark Fork Rivers.

Meanwhile to the west, when the Nez Perce were ordered by the U.S. Army to a small Idaho reservation in 1877, things did not remain so peaceful. Several young men lashed out, killing white settlers and sparking an ill-fated war. Nez Perce men, women, and children fled into the mountains, beginning a four-month, thirteen-hundred-mile flight through some of the most rugged terrain on the continent, in search of freedom and a place to live in peace.

Their course took them east over Lolo Trail, where they handily sidestepped soldiers from three-week-old Fort Missoula. Chief Joseph later recounted making "a treaty with these soldiers . . . that we might pass through the Bitter Root country in peace." After bypassing "Fort Fizzle," as it became known, the Nez Perce moved into the Bitterroot. While panicked residents sought shelter at Forts Owen and Missoula, and in hastily built sod forts at Corvallis and Skalkaho, the Nez Perce traveled south, hugging the river's quieter western shores. Despite appeals from the Nez Perce, the Salish and Pend d'Oreilles helped to keep the peace in the valley. After gathering supplies in Stevensville, the Nez Perce camped at Ross' Hole, then pushed up and over seven-thousand-foot Gibbon's Pass.

Believing they had outrun misfortune, they took refuge in the Big Hole Valley. Four days later, bad luck overtook them

Members of the Salish tribe pose here on October 15, 1891, the day of their departure to the Jocko Valley, with General Henry Carrington, who enforced their removal. On the far right sit Chief Charlot's wife and daughter. Carrington stands at right center. MHS Photo Archives

when General Howard's men, tracing their trail through the Bitterroot, awakened the camp with a dawn ambush. The Battle of the Big Hole left many dead and any lingering hopes the Nez Perce held for returning home shattered. They finally surrendered four months later after the Bear's Paw battle, just forty miles shy of the Canadian border.

Twelve years later, in 1889, the weary Charlot acknowledged the same reality when he consented to lead his beleaguered people to the Jocko reservation. On an October day in 1891 the last of the Salish began the long trip north.

JEWEL OF THE BITTERROOT

More than a dozen farmers had found their way to Fort Owen by 1860, along with explorers and traders, blacksmiths and millers, carpenters and harness makers. In 1863 the town of Stevensville was born just south of the fort, and from there farmers edged deeper into the valley, where the largest settlement, in the rich bottomlands at the mouth of Willow Creek, became known as Corvallis—Heart of the Valley.

The farmers of the Bitterroot catered almost entirely to the thousands of hungry miners in the gold camps. It was a two-week round-trip to the Grasshopper diggings at Bannack or the Stinking Water mines at Virginia City, and Bitterroot "squash peddlers" began hauling their crops and beef cattle around the mountains just as soon as they were big enough to sell. Early farming was almost as risky as mining, as farmers battled grasshoppers and bad weather, but demand for fresh vegetables was tremendous and the payoff was high.

In 1867 the first thousand Bitterroot Valley apple saplings were planted on the Fort Owen ranch, only to be devoured by grasshoppers before the season's end. The following spring Thomas Harris planted the valley's first successful apple trees, destined one day to become the orchard of Pine Grove near present-day Stevensville.

When the year 1870 rolled around, the census's head count of the valley's population stood at just over three hundred. In 1871 seven farm families just south of present-day Hamilton banded together to build the Big Corral, enclosing eleven hundred acres. The pole-fence corral, brainchild of Warren E. Harris to keep livestock in and unwanted visitors out, lasted

Horse-drawn wagons and sleds were used for the intensive logging of the Bitterroot Valley, which began during the 1880s with completion of the railroads and establishment of local sawmills. UM

about ten years. Today the Elliot House (site 46), with its hundred-year-old maple trees, and the century-old junipers at the Doran Farm (site 47) both date from the 1870s, the era of the Big Corral.

The 1880s saw great change in the Bitterroot Valley, as roads and railways, farms and timber camps carved indelibly into the face of the land. In 1883 the long-awaited Northern Pacific Railroad snaked its way across Montana, linking east with west at Gold Creek. Grading began on a Bitterroot branch line in July 1887, and the Missoula & Bitter Root Valley Railroad was completed to Grantsdale in June 1888.

The construction of the railroad opened the doorway to millions of acres of timber. The valley's sawmills increased production to meet burgeoning statewide demand, with the lion's share of the lumber (some 700,000 board feet per year) going to the booming cities of Butte, Anaconda, and Helena.

The founding father of Hamilton, Marcus Daly created the company town to fuel the Anaconda Company's voracious appetite for lumber. MHS Photo Archives

James Hedge, a veteran sawyer, ran one of the larger mills at River Siding (now the northern edge of Hamilton). The biggest mill of all was financed by Marcus Daly, the famed copper baron who owned half of the mines in Butte and the entire smelter town of Anaconda.

An Irishman who came to the New World in 1856, Marcus O'Daly stepped from the boat in New York at age fifteen with just the clothes on his back. He ventured west, first to California, then to Nevada, and ultimately Montana, dropping the O' from his name along the way. Daly had a meteoric rags-to-riches career, parlaying a shrewd business sense, an affable personality, and magical luck into a fortune. Arriving in Butte in 1876 at the end of the silver boom, Daly saw the potential of the rich, vast copper veins that lay even deeper in his mine, the Anaconda. He quietly bought up surrounding claims where the silver had played out, set up equipment, and began digging for copper in earnest. Backed by three other successful, self-made capitalists—George Hearst, James B. Haggin, and Lloyd Tevis—Daly built a copper reduction smelter on Warm Springs Creek in 1883–84, twenty-six miles from Butte, and founded the town of Anaconda. Over the remainder of the nineteenth century, Marcus Daly drew a vast coppery fortune from the prodigious Anaconda Mine, going down in history

Marcus Daly remodeled what had been a large farmhouse owned by Anthony Chaffin into this imposing Shingle-style residence (site 3). The house featured the typical irregular rooflines, round arches, grouped windows, sturdy porches, and the courses of shingles that gave this style its name. Radically remodeled a second time in 1909, it is now a fine museum. MHS Photo Archives

as the mightiest copper king to reign over the rollicking cities of Butte and Anaconda, and the infant state of Montana.

Daly had traversed the Bitterroot in 1864 and had been struck by this valley where wild grasses grew taller than a man's head. A shrewd opportunist, he probably noted that the open bench lands east of the river held promise for farming and that the valley as well contained some of the finest, densest stands of fir and pine in the territory. Two decades later, his fortune secure, Daly's long-held dream to return to the Bitterroot became reality.

Daly first purchased the homestead of Anthony Chaffin (one of the original Corvallis-area settlers) and surrounding farmland in 1886, launching the Bitter Root Stock Farm, which ultimately rolled across more than twenty-six thousand acres of fertile valley bench lands. A few years later Daly remodeled the Chaffin farmhouse into a fabulous country mansion (site 3), built a carriage house, greenhouses, barns, and stables and set about raising thoroughbred racehorses and standardbred trotters. Daly's Stock Farm was near a small settlement initially called Sanders Crossing; it became known as River Siding during the railroad years and later yet, Haggin, after Daly's loyal partner.

Daly modeled his stock farm after royal estates in Ireland and the Haggin horse farms of verdant Kentucky. His blueblooded thoroughbreds lived a life of luxury. For his prize racehorse Tammany, Daly built what was unquestionably the most stylish stable in Montana, a two-story brick barn with Colonial cupolas and Romanesque arches named Tammany's Castle (site 4). An outdoor track, a half-mile indoor winter

Marcus Daly built a stable that lived up to its name—Tammany's Castle (site 4)—for his favorite thoroughbred racehorse, Tammany, pictured on the left. MHS Photo Archives

training track, and a top-notch veterinary hospital completed the spread.

With the Anaconda Company's mines and smelter booming, Daly also chose the upper Bitterroot as the site for milling the million board feet of lumber that his company needed each year. He began to purchase timberlands in the valley, buying from the railroad, the federal government, and other valley property owners. Daly soon controlled thousands of acres of rich primeval forest land.

Daly had his eye on the Grantsdale area near the Stock Farm for a big lumber mill; there he would create a millpond by damming the Bitterroot River near the mouth of Skalkaho Creek. The dam was to be a modern affair with ice breakers and fish ladders. Daly secured the needed land and in November 1889 contracted "Messrs. Brennan and Hamilton" to manage a sawmill brought in for the interim while the dam and the Big Mill were being built. By year's end the Brennan mill was producing lumber for new homes in Grantsdale, and soon almost all the sawyers in the Bitterroot were cutting for Marcus Daly.

Needing a place for mill workers to live, Daly then approached H. H. Grant, founding father of Grantsdale, to purchase the townsite outright. Legend holds that when Grant demanded a steep price, Daly cursed him in a rage, "You go to hell. I'll see grass grow in the streets of Grantsdale."

Daly turned to his engineer and front man, James W. Hamilton, and his lawyer, Robert A. O'Hara, to organize his own town. By denying affiliation with Daly, Hamilton managed to buy a total of 160 acres for a townsite from several nearby landowners. Hamilton generously laid the town out with amply wide, eighty-foot streets, forty-nine square blocks, and 1032 building lots. The Bitter Root Development Company was officially incorporated on August 12, 1890, and a month later, on September 4, it filed the plat for the new town named after the man who sparked it to life. James Hamilton transferred ownership to Daly shortly thereafter, and Robert O'Hara was elected mayor.

Almost immediately the population surged. After a three-hour rail trip over the forty-seven miles between Missoula and Hamilton, a reporter in 1894 complained of frequent "vexatious delays" to load freight on the one daily train. But arriving in Hamilton he was impressed by the town's "liveliness" and that when the train pulled in each evening, "a large percentage of the 700 souls who inhabit the bustling little city turn out to welcome its arrival."

The town blanketed the lowlands east of the river, and Main Street reached between the town's most vital organs—the railroad and the mill. Daly's Bitter Root Development

Hamilton's development depended upon the railroad. Here the Northern Pacific's branch line, the Missoula & Bitter Root Valley Railroad, stops at the Hamilton depot, once the town's most significant building. MHS Photo Archives

Company owned the town—the townsite, company homes, the Big Mill, a huge company store, and a hotel. The company managers lived in large homes on the south side of town. "Nearly all the available gentlemen of the city" were members of the Bitter Root Development Company's Valley Club, located in two large rooms "fitted up in an elaborate manner" upstairs from the company store.

Off Main Street the three hundred mill workers, who bent their backs to the daily task of keeping the mill humming, lived in cottages knotted tightly together in the shadow of the mill. A wide wooden boardwalk lined Main Street from the mill to the neighborhoods, and children and wives in the homes would know it was noon dinnertime or quitting time "by the noise the many heavy boots made as their wearers— hardy men all—plodded east from their work."

Business folk plied their trade in a five-block town center along Main, Front, and Second Streets, in one- to two-story buildings of wood, brick, and stone. In September 1890 Patrick Cone opened a brickyard west of town. With 250,000 bricks ready to lay and another 500,000 in the works, the *Western News* challenged Cone to "give us plenty of brick till we build up this one man's town, which we are proud of."

The town grew while timber crews slashed their way through the length of the Bitterroot. In May 1891 20 million feet of logs clogged the river awaiting the first mill season at Hamilton. Completed in September 1892, the Big Mill at full throttle turned out a whopping 35 million board feet per year. Most of the 200,000 feet of lumber milled there daily was piled onto railcars and sent to build the Butte mines and fuel the Anaconda smelter.

Following a scandal in which Bitter Root Development Company lumber crews were caught with $3.4 million in timber

The Anaconda Company's Big Mill at Hamilton was a sprawling operation, with a big pond, sawmill, lath mill, sash and door factory, and planer. BVHS

illegally cut on federal lands, Daly shut it down and transferred its operations to his Anaconda Copper Mining Company in 1894. Through the late 1890s Anaconda Company timbering continued to boom. The company added the Big Blackfoot Milling Company at Bonner and a new mill at St. Regis to its operation and locked up the remaining major timber stands in the Bitterroot. At the century's turn, with seventeen hundred loggers and lumber workers and a total output approaching 200 million board feet per year, Daly was heralded as "perhaps the biggest lumber manufacturer in the world."

At the Bitter Root Stock Farm, two hundred to three hundred workers were employed, raising horses, cattle, grain, vegetables, and orchards. Many of these crops were shipped by rail along with lumber to the mine and smelter workers in Butte and Anaconda. During the 1890s the Northern Pacific ran a train—the Copper Limited—between Hamilton and Butte.

Homes were built for the Stock Farm's superintendent, foreman, veterinarian, and creamery manager. Daly established the Pioneer Creamery—Montana's first—in 1896, which made in-town deliveries and daily shipments to Butte and Anaconda. In 1895 Ravalli County erected a fairgrounds (site 2) at the border between the farm and the town. Each year at the fair Stock Farm produce and horse racing were among the main attractions.

Hamilton grew steadily through the Gay Nineties. By 1893 the town boasted over forty businesses, including three public halls and four hotels. To this total Marcus Daly added the sumptuous Ravalli Hotel, the Ravalli County Bank, and an opera house (only the bank—site 15—remains today). Twenty-one saloons on Main Street and a red-light district known as the "Bad Lands" along N. Fourth Street, catered to lumberjacks, sawyers, businessmen, and Stock Farm hands. Most of the Bad Lands's "female boarding houses"—a common euphemism for brothels—burned in 1908; local police shut down the remaining brothels in 1915.

By April 1898 when the Ravalli County county seat came to rest in Hamilton, the town was well established. For two years, while A. J. Gibson designed a courthouse befitting the new county, county offices were based in the Lucas Opera House. Upon completion in 1900 the courthouse (site 31, see photograph page 53) became the crown jewel of the town. With its stately Romanesque brick and granite design and lofty tower, it marked the southeast corner of Hamilton's business district.

As the calendar turned to 1900, census takers tallied 1,257 citizens in the town of Hamilton. Later that year Marcus Daly died suddenly. While many in Hamilton felt "his passing as a personal loss," he was eulogized in newspapers the country over: "Marcus Daly is dead and peace to his ashes"—New York *Telegraph;* "Marcus Daly was Irish and all the name implies"

—Detroit *Tribune*; "He was a man of warm and generous heart, a staunch friend and a frank, open enemy"—Denver *News*. Shortly thereafter Daly's wife Margaret auctioned off all the racehorses—including the legendary Tammany—in New York's Madison Square Garden. Production at the Big Mill slowed, and the future of the town looked cloudy.

LAND OF APPLES AND OPPORTUNITY

> "In a few years the stump wastes are bound
> to be transformed into fine farms and orchards."
> —*Western Lumberman*, 1900

Behind timber crews who stripped the forest from the Bitterroot Valley floor, farmers followed, sowing and seeding the freshly cleared acres. The surge in farming went hand in hand with the steel girding of the west by the railroads and the waves of passengers that the trains carried westward.

To grow crunchy apples and plump berries, farmers had to have water and lots of it. Rainfall in the Bitterroot Valley (about twelve inches a year on average) was just not enough. Crop irrigation dated to the first farmers in the valley—the missionaries at St. Mary's. Then, in 1887, the first irrigation ditch—the Ward-Galloway Ditch—was built to water the bench lands between Gird and Willow creeks. That same year, farmers planted over a thousand fruit saplings in the Bitterroot. On his Stock Farm, Marcus Daly had several ditches dug with award-winning results. Daly's blooming orchards, golden grain fields, acres of sun-drenched vegetables, four-foot cabbages, sleek horses, and fattened cows all showcased the potential of a well-watered valley farm.

Images of plenty, such as this one of ⟨✧⟩ lure investors to the Bitterroot Valley children deluged by apples, helped ⟨|⟩ in the 1910s. MHS Photo Archives

Over the years farmers and land speculators dug other ditches, which were followed by more orchards and farms. Alongside newly milled lumber, fruit crates became a standard part of the Big Mill's production. In the late 1890s, Daly ramrodded an effort to knit all his existing ditches into one enormous network. The Daly Ditch branched from Skalkaho Creek ten miles above Grantsdale and meandered through Stock Farm fields from horizon to horizon. Completed after Daly's death by F. A. Jones (chief engineer) and H. S. Lord, it was forty-three miles long in all, making it the state's largest at that time.

The pace of Hamilton slowed in the wake of Daly's death and shutdown of some of his Bitterroot operations. But a few years later a grand land scheme, linking a vast irrigation ditch with farm development, again boosted the fortunes of the town. Picking up where Daly's canal left off, the Big Ditch was launched in 1905 by the Dinsmore Irrigation and Development Corporation. Samuel Dinsmore's starry-eyed goal was to build an eighty-mile ditch from Lake Como to Stevensville.

The $1.5 million plan sparked local enthusiasm but fell onto hard times the very next year. Rescued when a partnership of local investors and Chicago financiers pumped in twice the money, the new Bitterroot District Irrigation Company planned to line the ditch with apple orchards. In 1905, after the company was reborn a final time as the Bitterroot Valley Irrigation Company, fifty vertical feet were added to the Como Dam, and the digging began. Surveyors' tapes unfurled along both sides of the ditch, as twenty-five thousand soon-to-be-dampened acres along its route were split into ten- and twenty-acre orchard tracts.

A Mike Mulligan–style steam shovel dubbed Li'l Giant bit into the earth at Lake Como and never looked back. Munching its way down the valley, Li'l Giant left in its wake a canal twenty-four feet wide, to carry a stream six feet deep. The shovel scooted along steel rails laid just ahead of its path—up and down gullies, around foothills, across trestles. When one of the trestles collapsed under the steam shovel, it took several weeks, fifteen teams of horses, and a huge Anaconda Company logging wagon to put the shovel back on track.

By 1909 the canal reached to Burnt Fork Creek, and orchard sales began. Hopeful easterners were sold preplanted orchards with promises that an easy life picking apples, cherries, pears, or plums awaited them in this "Land of Opportunity." The promoters made big money from the arrangement. Even before water trickled into the ditch in 1910, apple boomers flocked to the valley, paying up to a thousand dollars per acre on land once worth a few dollars per acre. Some purchased just one

Fired with cordwood and coal that
was trucked in on horse-drawn
wagons, the steam shovel Li'l Giant
excavated an irrigation canal that
stretched from Lake Como to
Stevensville. BVHS

tract, others strung many together, like the Thousand Acre
Orchard near Corvallis. Two orchards—Como Orchards and
Sunset Orchards—ran over sixteen hundred acres, rivaling any
in the Pacific Northwest. McIntosh Reds found their way from
the Bitterroot to tables as far away as New York City, and for a
time the apple growers prospered.

The land rush in the valley rekindled Hamilton's economy
and population growth. The population swelled to over three
thousand, and a new addition to the town was platted in 1910
by Big Ditch investors. Named Pine Grove after the valley's
original apple orchards, the addition stretched across twenty-
two blocks on the south end of town. Gradually Hamilton

acquired a more picturesque appearance as streets were paved and lighted and shade trees and landscaping were added to the roadways.

Talented architects of the day were brought in to design buildings in Hamilton, A. J. Gibson and H. E. "Kirk" Kirkemo from Missoula, Charles Bell and John Kent from Helena, and A. F. Heide of Washington among them. In the Bitterroot's fruit belt, the celebrated architect Frank Lloyd Wright was tapped to design a garden community at Como Orchards and the town of Bitterroot in 1908–9. These recreation communities were to feature summer homes and clubhouses; the planners hoped to draw midwestern city dwellers to summer or retire under Montana's big skies.

The booming Bitterroot Valley attracted others with farm dreams. In 1916 local papers announced a "sugar plant for the Bitter Root," touting the Montana-Utah Sugar Company's plan to turn beets into sugar right on the outskirts of Hamilton. No doubt eyeing the success of sugar beet refineries in Billings and Missoula, the Hamilton Chamber of Commerce contracted local farmers to plant over ten thousand acres in beets the following spring. Local schoolchildren were paid $1.50 a day to help with cultivation. In early 1917 building of the beet plant began, smokestack first (site 1). The stack rose to a height of eighty-five feet before the bottom fell out of the company; by year's end the Montana-Utah Sugar Company was dead. Bitterroot farmers trucked their beets to Missoula that fall, and ever after the stack remained a sentinel to the beet plant that never was.

It was no exaggeration that "the Hood River and Wenatchee Valleys could be placed in the Bitter Root and there would still be room for another." But valley size alone did not guarantee fruit crops and profits, and by 1920 changing markets, killing frosts, and soil depletion spelled the limit, and then the end, of the apple era.

FEVER IN THE MOUNTAINS

Hamilton bloomed again, unexpectedly, during the 1920s and 1930s as researchers became locked in combat against a fatal disease that arose in the Bitterroot. "Black measles" or "spotted fever" was a fatal bacterial fever carried by small mammals and spread by ticks. Isolated in the valley's stony side canyons, the disease was unleashed during the logging of the valley and its foothills by unknowing Bitterroot lumberjacks.

First recorded in the southern Bitterroot in 1873, the number of cases of spotted fever rose alarmingly through the next quarter century, especially among ranchers, timber workers, and others who worked in the mountain foothills. Blamed on drinking snowmelt water or on sawdust piles at the lumber mills, the dreaded fever claimed the lives of 80 percent of those who contracted it.

As the new century turned, the people of the valley appealed to the newly formed Montana State Board of Health, and doctors Earle Strain and Albert F. Longeway were dispatched to study the epidemic. In 1902 researchers identified the epicenters as the west side of the Bitterroot River and along the Snake River in Idaho. Dr. Strain and colleagues suggested that the disease was insect borne, implicating ticks and ground squirrels as the primary carriers.

In 1906 Dr. H. T. Ricketts of the U.S. Public Health Service pitched a canvas tent on the lawn of a Missoula hospital, and in this makeshift lab he proved conclusively that Rocky Mountain spotted fever spread from infected animals to humans through tick bites. Under the microscope Ricketts identified the bacterium; he then managed to culture the disease in guinea pigs and monkeys. Shortly thereafter, not far from Hamilton, a field station to study the disease in the wild was established in 1910 in a cabin on tick-ridden Sweeney Creek. The cabin, deserted since its owner had died there of the fever, was dubbed Camp Venustus (the wood tick's Latin name).

Tick-control programs kicked off during the 1910s. Wooden dipping vats throughout the Bitterroot were filled with an arsenic solution, and the dipping—of cattle, horses, sheep, goats, "even ranch dogs"—became mandatory. Many in the valley opposed the program; farmers were reluctant to subject their animals to the arsenic plunge, and apple boom speculators feared publicity that would drive down real estate values.

In 1911 Dr. Thomas McClintic, who was heading up the dipping program, died of spotted fever. Two years later two boys came down with the fever after hand spraying their father's blooded mares. As Carl Wemple remembered, "My brother died; I spent 54 days packed in ice but still running a fever. Someone blew up the dipping vat with a whole case of dynamite."

The control program slowed but did not stop the spread of spotted fever. A vaccine was sorely needed. Finally, in 1924, working in the abandoned Canyon Creek Schoolhouse, Dr. R. R. Spencer of the U.S. Public Health Service and state entomologist Dr. Ralph R. Parker formulated one. Inoculating themselves first, they turned the tide on the fever. When the disease turned up in the other Rocky Mountain states, they were ready with the new vaccine. (The schoolhouse is now home to the Hamilton Playhouse, 100 Ricketts Rd.)

The Canyon Creek lab became the site of vaccine manufacture, which involved raising millions of infected ticks. It was dangerous work. During the 1920s alone, eleven of sixteen

The Rocky Mountain Laboratory (site 45) was built in the stately Collegiate Gothic style, marked by medieval motifs on the vestibule and the crenellated parapet (the low wall on the roof that was furnished with battlements). Later buildings on the site repeated this pattern. BVHS

workers in the lab contracted spotted fever or tularemia, another disease transmitted through insect bites. Three of them—William Gettinger, Henry Cowan, and Albert LeRoy Curlee—died. In 1927 the Montana legislature set aside funds to build a new medical research lab, larger and safer, in Hamilton.

The Rocky Mountain Laboratory (site 45) was completed in May 1928. Three years later spotted fever turned up in the East, and the U.S. Public Health Service bought the lab from the state and expanded it. Working at the lab in 1938, Dr. Herald R. Cox discovered that the spotted fever vaccine could be cultured in the yolks of live chicken eggs. Cox's breakthrough forever changed the way that vaccines are cultured, and the days of rearing ticks by the millions were over.

During World War II the Rocky Mountain Laboratory focused its research on combating diseases that raged in wartime

Europe. The Rocky Mountain Laboratory produced a half million doses of typhoid vaccine in 1942 alone and, in 1945, over 3 million doses of yellow fever vaccine.

Following the war and the development of broad-spectrum "cure-all" antibiotics, the research role of the Rocky Mountain Laboratory was downgraded, and many of its functions moved to newer, larger national labs. The lab continues as a venue of scientific research, however, and its historic significance was commemorated when the complex was listed in the National Register of Historic Places in 1988.

Mirror on the Town

⊬≡⊣

DOWNTOWN BUILDINGS

When James Hamilton sowed the seeds for the Hamilton townsite on behalf of his employer Marcus Daly, he planted it solidly between the steel rails of the Bitter Root & Missoula Railroad and the Big Mill. Conceived as a perfect square, the town of Hamilton sprouted along the lines of a compass. Within the square, a geometric universe unfolded like a big quilt made of forty-nine equal blocks. In this pattern, north-south streets were numbered and cinched together by east-west streets with more colorful names: River, Pine, Cherry, Pinckney, Main, State, Bedford, and Madison. Running right up the center was the town's Main Street, joining First Street at the tracks to form a T-shaped grid. The T-shape plan was a common hallmark of western railroad towns during this era, and in Hamilton the T had the added feature of the Big Mill at its base.

Along the streets of Hamilton, buildings sprang up in phases—hammers and saws going full tilt during the good years, dying away to nothing during harder times. Hamilton's First Street ran straight along the railroad tracks, and along the town's east side a typical railroad zone developed with warehouses, liveries, and a grain elevator looming above it all. The town's businesses elbowed one another for choice spots along Main Street (which linked the railroad to the mill) and Second Street. Here a person could find most of life's comforts—meats, beer, and candy; boots, dresses, and caps; saddles, books, and blankets; haircuts and hot baths. And, at the end of a long day, a bed for the night.

During Hamilton's infancy, buildings were small and quickly built; a few were even hauled to town on railcars. With plenty of lumber being milled right on the edge of town, the homes and stores in Hamilton featured lots of wood. Those in the early business district had the look of the Old West, with crude, rectangular, gable-roofed buildings hiding behind more stylish false fronts. Only two or three of those first-generation buildings still stand; the rest were replaced as the town grew.

Marcus Daly's plan for a successful (and profitable) company town included the ubiquitous company store. Daly's was

The view up Main Street in the late 1890s revealed numerous false-front buildings, designed to give an instantly urban feel to a small town. Home to *Western News* when erected in 1895, the Art City Building at 407 W. Main **(site 13)** is Hamilton's last well-preserved false-front store. BVHS

The Ravalli Hotel is pictured here ca. 1905, approximately ten years after it was built for the sum of thirty-five thousand dollars. Until it burned down in 1919, the Colonial Revival–style hotel invited tourists to "come and spend the summer with us. The Bitter Root invites you and the Ravalli will see to creature comforts"— sumptuous accommodations, elegant dining, bicycle riding, and livery stables. MHS Photo Archives

two stories in height, built of brick, and designed to sell the goods. It was located where the Bower Building (site 17) now stands. As observed by a news reporter in 1894, a "tour down the broad main thoroughfare finds the wanderer gazing into the massive show windows of the Bitter Root Development company's [Anaconda Company] store, the foremost commercial and financial institution of the county." Embellishing upon this initial effort, Daly upped the architectural ante, adding three prominent brick buildings to the 1890s skyline. The Ravalli Hotel and Ravalli County Bank (site 15) carried a weighty message of permanence and stability, helping to anchor the fledgling downtown. And the Lucas Opera House (named for Sam Lucas, Daly's thoroughbred foreman) introduced an air of culture to this town in the woods.

The late-nineteenth-century look of downtown Hamilton was matter-of-factly functional, and during the 1890s locally manufactured materials predominated. Increasingly, town builders chose brick and stone. They knew too well the risk of fire that came from mixing oil lamps and wood stoves with tinder-dry wooden buildings. From brickyards on the edges of town came the low-fire, red-brown brick that was used for many downtown buildings. In addition to brick, masons laid a bluish gray volcanic stone—advertised at the time as "far superior to brick"—quarried in Corvallis. James Barr, a Corvallis builder, sawed slabs of this stone for buildings around the area.

Style was not left by the wayside, however, even on the earliest false-front buildings. And on the masonry blocks there

When Marcus Daly first built his Anaconda Company department store in the heart of downtown **(site 17)**, the building dominated the commercial landscape. It continued to do so for almost half a century until it was destroyed by fire in 1936. MHS Library

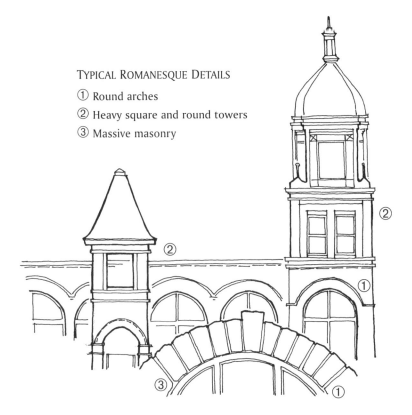

TYPICAL ROMANESQUE DETAILS
① Round arches
② Heavy square and round towers
③ Massive masonry

were often hints of late Victorian styles such as Italianate and Renaissance. These influences were visible on buildings like the Anaconda Company's department store.

After 1900 downtown architecture (both commercial and public) took a turn toward the progressive, reflecting twentieth-century tastes and the town's apple-grown affluence. Buildings of this era dressed in higher style and loomed larger on the streetscape. The Romanesque style had a heavy look, with trademark round arches and rough-hewn stone. It was featured on the Ravalli County Bank (site 15) in the late 1890s, reappeared on the county courthouse (site 31, see photograph page 53), and was echoed on the city hall (site 23, see photograph page 54).

Where early business houses occupied single building lots, those built after 1900 often filled two or more lots. Hamilton business leaders hired talented Montana architects to design new

In 1910 Frank Drinkenberg and partners built both the First National Bank Building (at right, **site 24**) and the matching commercial block (at left), which housed the Ravalli County Mercantile Company. Between them stood the Perkins and Doran Shop, which later became the Star and then the Liberty Theater. BVHS

downtown business blocks, and they set the pace with buildings to last through the new century. Missoula-based architect A. J. Gibson led the way in Hamilton with designs that relied upon high-fire brick, metal mullion storefronts, and leaded-glass transoms, all imported by rail. Frank Drinkenberg's 1910 First National Bank (**site 24**) and two sister buildings by Gibson—the Bitter Root Stock Farm Office built in 1909 (**site 25**) and the McGrath Block built in 1910 (**site 16**)—are among the best examples. Gibson's buildings use the same design formula, although the Neo-Classical motifs on the entrance and cornice of the McGrath Building set it apart from its plainer sisters.

In the 1930s Hamilton builders became enamored with Modernism. H. H. Kirkemo, a protégé of Gibson and his successor

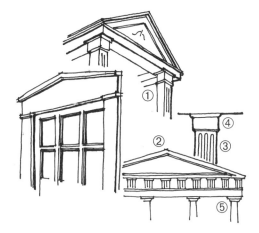

TYPICAL NEOCLASSICAL DETAILS

① Portico (porch)
② Triangular pediment
③ Pilasters (columns engaged in walls)
④ Capitals
⑤ Tall, light-colored columns

Ole Bakke, was at the forefront of this movement that dropped parts of the downtown skyline to a single story, particularly along Main Street. Beginning with the Ravalli County Creamery in 1933 (site 12), the Art Moderne style appeared, with its low horizontal profile, polychrome brickwork, and sharp-edged geometry.

The Art Moderne–style Ravalli County Creamery (site 12) was built in two parts and at one time was covered with a luxuriant growth of climbing ivy. The east portion (at right) opened first, in 1933, seven years after John Howe moved his creamery from Stevensville to Hamilton. The west portion was added in 1946. BVHS

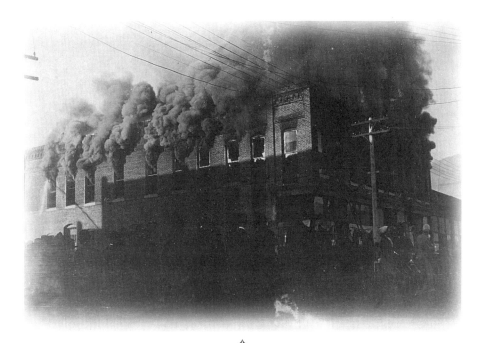

The Anaconda Company department store burned twice after it became Valley Mercantile; the first fire in October 1910 is pictured here; a second fire in 1936 destroyed the building. BVHS

Built in 1936, the Bower Building (site 17) replaced the Anaconda Company store; the new department store boasted modern lines, smooth, buff-colored brick, and dark-chocolate brick banding. BVHS

Three years later, when the Valley Mercantile (the new name of Daly's Anaconda Company store) burned down in a roaring blaze, the Bower Building (site 17) arose from the embers wearing the long, sleek look of the twentieth century. Riding the same Modernist bandwagon down Main Street were the Roxy Theater (site 11) with an Art Deco flair to its polychrome brick, its next-door neighbor Ford's Clothing (site 18), and the Telephone Exchange Building (site 14), spare but for its round-arched entrance.

HOMES

Hamilton was born a lumber town, and it grew with every turn of the mill blades. Martha Allison, owner of a ranch just north of the Hamilton town limits, made the first addition to Hamilton in 1891. The Riverview Addition contained twelve blocks and streets named for her Empire State heritage—New York, Adirondac, Saranac. Hamilton's north end took on the character of a working-class neighborhood, with clusters of mill worker cottages, one-story wooden homes capped by pyramid-shaped roofs. Two large boarding houses—Geyer and Burke—sat on prominent corners, where the mill workers passed them every day. The neighborhood filled quickly, and three years later Martha (Allison) Reinkeh (remarried by this time) greatly expanded Riverview to cover a total area of forty-one blocks.

The Bitter Root Development Company, meanwhile, expanded the town south in 1894. The resulting Southside Addition became the neighborhood of choice, the place where company managers and bank presidents built their homes. South Fifth garnered the most affluent Hamiltonians, and the

HAMILTON
TOWNSITE AND ADDITIONS

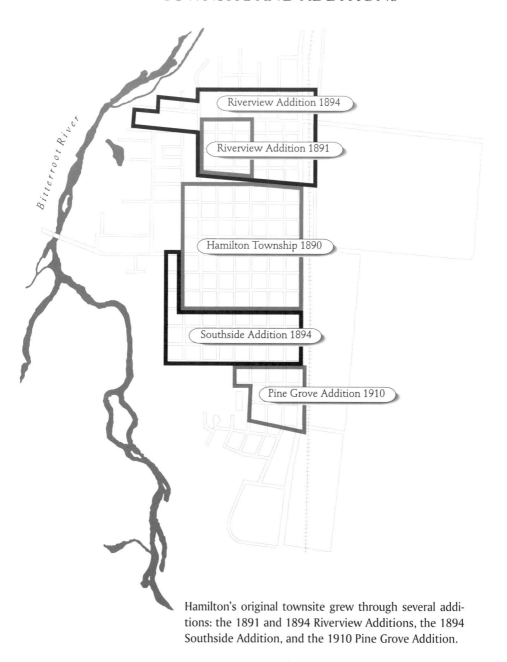

Riverview Addition 1894

Riverview Addition 1891

Hamilton Township 1890

Southside Addition 1894

Pine Grove Addition 1910

Bitterroot River

Hamilton's original townsite grew through several additions: the 1891 and 1894 Riverview Additions, the 1894 Southside Addition, and the 1910 Pine Grove Addition.

Pictured ca. 1900, the A. H. Geyer Boarding House, at S. Fourth and State Streets, was home to many Anaconda Company mill workers. A long table in the first-floor dining room sat twenty to thirty boarders; the upstairs was divided into bedrooms. BVHS

large homes that raised up along the street announced the good fortunes of their occupants.

The homes of Hamilton ranged from basic to pretentious. Company housing for Hamilton's mill workers was the standard fare of nineteenth-century factory towns. Across industrialized America, boxy, pyramidal-roofed, four-square workers' houses rested in the shadows of factories and mills. In Hamilton, it was the mighty Anaconda Company that built many such cottages and rented them to those workers unable to afford other housing. Throughout Hamilton one can spot them still, these one-story homes with a central entrance from an open porch, four rooms, and varying amounts of Queen Anne–style embellishment (site 35). These houses clung to tight lots, but in their yards residents found room to grow gardens, hang clothing, and raise chickens.

This little four-square cottage is typical of Anaconda Company workers' housing in early Hamilton, with its boxy form, pyramidal, hipped roof, and open front porch. Today, several homes along the 500 block of S. Fourth **(site 35)** reflect this early building style. BVHS

Intermixed with workers' cottages, company housing for mill managers anchored a neighborhood of more well-to-do, professional types. Now a National Register Historic District, Hamilton's Southside reflected the affluence of the young town. Yards were larger here; two and three lots were often ganged together for one home. In this neighborhood, large trees and flowering shrubs ornament many lawns, and the houses often feature outbuildings: carriage houses, barns, sheds, garages, and an occasional outhouse.

At the helm of the Anaconda Company, Marcus Daly controlled an army of carpenters from Anaconda who knew their way around the styles of the day and built many homes in the popular Queen Anne and Colonial Revival styles. They set to fleshing out the town, filling the neighborhoods with housing

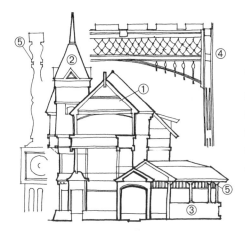

TYPICAL QUEEN ANNE DETAILS

① Irregular roofline/floor plan
② Towers, turrets
③ Wraparound porches
④ Fancy trim
⑤ Decorative porch posts
   and spindles

for both mill workers and professional company employees. The W. W. McCrackin House (site 27) and the similar C. M. Crutchfield House (site 32) were both built in the 1890s by "Daly's carpenters," as they were called, and are elegant examples of high Queen Anne style. The McCrackin House was built originally for an upper-level Anaconda Company manager, but apparently the young manager's wife convinced him to live elsewhere, and it was sold to Ravalli County Bank president McCrackin. Two blocks away "Colonel" C. M. Crutchfield's house took six long months to complete—it was built on Sundays, by the carpentry team Daly assigned to build the town's First Christian Church (site 39) the other six days of the week. Crutchfield was the Anaconda Company's lead attorney in Hamilton.

Martha Reinkeh lived in a Queen Anne–style farmhouse, probably the oldest house in town (site 5). At odds to the building lot, the house (built ca. 1880) appears to have stood solidly in its place before Reinkeh platted the Riverview Additions on the north side of the Hamilton townsite. As well as being a major landowner in Hamilton, Woodside, and Victor, Reinkeh was known as a cantankerous eccentric. She often traveled in a goat-drawn cart until her goat was shot after it butted a businessman through the Victor hardware store window.

With its vertical, irregular massing, steep gable roof, and variety of siding and spindle work, Mayor W. W. McCrackin's home **(site 27)**, built in 1892, was one of Hamilton's finest Queen Anne houses. A three-stall carriage barn with tall cupola matches the residence. BVHS

Martha Reinkeh's home **(site 5)** appears to be the oldest house in the town, dating to ca. 1880. Behind the home today stands an octagonal tower that once capped the viewing stand overlooking Marcus Daly's racetrack. Inset, top left, is a picture of Reinkeh. BVHS

Frank H. Drinkenberg, an associate of Reinkeh, was the real estate entrepreneur credited in news reports of the day as largely responsible for platting the Riverview Additions. Purchasing large swaths of Riverview property when it was still open grassland, Drinkenberg sold lots and built several homes to spur development of the neighborhood. His own home, built in 1895, was Hamilton's first brick house of substance (site 6). Drinkenberg became president of Hamilton's First National Bank, four-term mayor, and owner of several downtown business blocks.

Marcus Daly seems to have been the local champion of Shingle-style architecture, a style popular during the last two decades of the nineteenth century. The Shingle style borrowed

Banker/real estate developer Frank Drinkenberg's home in the Riverview Addition (site 6) was built in Queen Anne style. Note its jaunty octagonal turret, complicated roof, and graceful woodwork, all traditional Queen Anne elements. This historic view also depicts the graceful, open veranda that was removed in later years. BVHS

freely from ornate Victorian styles to create a more rustic and straightforward aesthetic. Gone were the overly complex turrets, the fussy bric-a-brac, and the multicolored paint schemes. In their place Shingle style offered a more unified look, emphasizing simpler massing, rounded-off profiles, and sturdier proportions, all draped by row upon row of cedar shingles.

The finest Shingle homes in the area were built for Marcus Daly himself. Following a sweeping Shingle-style makeover of the Chaffin farmhouse on the Riverside stock farm (site 3, see photograph on page 11), the Dalys in 1890 built a second elegant home right in town (site 34). However, the family never lived there, choosing to spend their summers in the Bitterroot at their mansion, Riverside. Instead, the house served as the Bitter Root Development Office base of operations until 1895, after which time it was rented to various business associates.

Built originally for the Daly family, who never lived here, this Shingle-style home (site 34) instead served as the base of operations for the Bitter Root Development Office until 1895, when the offices moved to the newly completed Ravalli County Bank (site 15). SHPO

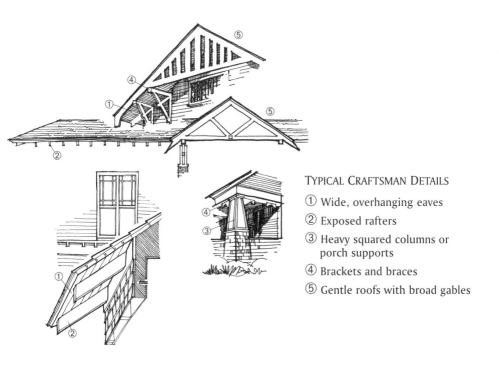

TYPICAL CRAFTSMAN DETAILS

① Wide, overhanging eaves
② Exposed rafters
③ Heavy squared columns or porch supports
④ Brackets and braces
⑤ Gentle roofs with broad gables

As the nineteenth century drew to a close, Hamilton neighborhoods were still fairly open, featuring large homes on corner lots interspersed with smaller homes and still-vacant lots. After 1900, with ditch water flowing and orchards blooming, Hamilton saw a new surge in home building. Although builders continued to refer to tried-and-true Victorian styles and four-square plans for a few more years, fresh new building styles soon colored the town in shades of Bungalow, Craftsman, and Prairie.

The apple boom years peaked during the heyday of the Arts and Crafts movement in American architecture and left an array of beautiful Craftsman homes across town. Spacious and sturdy with a tendency toward handcraft and naturalism, the Craftsman style sprang from the minds of California architects and brothers Henry S. and Charles M. Greene. The

The Robert Getty House **(site 41)** underscores the Japanese influences that helped inspire the Craftsman style, with its wide roof angles, curved rafters, and pagoda-like flare to the eaves. SHPO

purest example of Arts and Crafts design in Hamilton is the home of Dr. Robert Getty, built ca. 1912 **(site 41)**.

Born in the west, the Craftsman style emphasized functionality and connection with the environment and suited Montana's practicality and rugged surroundings. Many of

Many of Hamilton's larger Craftsman homes, like A. H. Downing's residence **(site 40)**, shared a distinctive boxy look, with steep side gables, recessed front porches, and large upper-level front dormers. SHPO

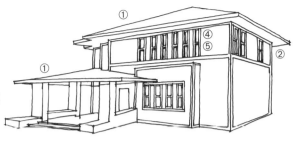

TYPICAL PRAIRIE STYLE DETAILS

① Low-pitched roofs, often hipped

② Large overhangs

③ Horizontal lines emphasized

④ Tall casement windows

⑤ Windows often grouped

Hamilton's larger Craftsman homes could be cousins; they share a distinctive tall, boxy look; steep, side-gabled roofs; recessed front porches; and large upper-level front dormers. Dating to 1910, A. H. Downing's bungalow (site 40) is one of the town's finest examples.

Popular simultaneously with the Craftsman, the Prairie style used organic design principles to blur the lines between building and nature. Created by Frank Lloyd Wright and other Chicago architects, this indigenous American style emphasized horizontal rhythms though the use of heavy bases, projecting hipped roofs, and banded windows. Inside, an open floor plan often revolved around a central fireplace. The Charles Hoffman House (site 44), built ca. 1914, is an excellent representative of Prairie-style architecture.

Also common during the early 1900s were Revival styles that revisited the proportions and decoration of past eras. Greek Revival, Colonial Revival, Dutch Revival, and Tudor Revival all put in appearances in Hamilton during the apple craze.

The Colonial Revival style was used on a wide variety of Hamilton buildings. Harkening to the building traditions of early America, Colonial Revival architecture has been in vogue in the United States off and on throughout the entire twentieth century. Hamilton is blessed with some very fine examples,

The banded windows, low-pitched hip roof, and wide eaves all lend a characteristic horizontality to | Charles Hoffman's Prairie home **(site 44)**, the only high-style example in Hamilton. SHPO

and Margaret Daly's 1909 Georgian-style Colonial makeover of the family's mansion **(site 3)** is by far the most extravagant.

The building of the Rocky Mountain Laboratory in 1928 spurred residential construction in Hamilton, but not without a fight. Residents of Hamilton's Pine Grove Addition, who

TYPICAL COLONIAL REVIVAL DETAILS

① Hipped roof

② Central portico

③ Symmetrical design

④ Accentuated front doorway often with sidelights and fanlights

Rebuilt in 1909 by Marcus Daly's widow Margaret, this Georgian–style Colonial-Revival mansion **(site 3)**, with its imposing classical portico and grand proportions, rivaled the most elegant homes in the state. MHS Photo Archives

feared becoming infected by Rocky Mountain spotted fever, sued the state (and lost) over the plan to place the lab in their neighborhood. Construction of the lab and the creation of new jobs kicked off a minor building boom during the 1930s, which helped again to revive the Colonial style. The twin residences built at the Rocky Mountain Laboratory in 1938–39 **(site 45)** and the 1930s-era makeover of the Bibler Apartments (originally the laundry and servants quarters for the Ravalli Hotel— site 29) are interesting residential examples, while Hamilton High School and Marcus Daly Memorial Hospital are stately examples of public Colonial Revival architecture at its best **(sites 26 and 28, see photographs on pages 55 and 58)**.

Picturesque Tudor Revival houses came onto the scene during the 1920s and 1930s. Conjuring up the quaint charm of English cottages, steep Tudor roof angles and curved lines on the entrances were suited to houses of all sizes. With trim

A picturesque form of Tudor Revival design gave homes of the 1920s and 1930s a storybook charm. Dr. George B. Taylor's home **(site 42)** displays the style's characteristic steep rooflines, half-timbering, tight-cropped eaves, prominent chimney, and stucco cladding trimmed with brick. It is the finest local example of the style and somewhat larger than most picturesque Tudor Revival homes. SHPO

shrubbery and Tudor half-timbering, Dr. George B. Taylor's 1935 home (site 42) paints a picture of Old World tranquility.

Balancing these nostalgic revival styles was the straight-ahead, no-nonsense look of American modernism. During its heyday in the 1930s, Art Moderne was less commonly used for residences, although its format was conceived as "a machine for living." In Hamilton, the Pine Apartment building, constructed ca. 1938 (site 43), embodies Art Moderne aesthetics. Howard Bates, a local businessman, built it to provide housing for the employees of the Rocky Mountain Laboratory.

While most of the homes in Hamilton were built of wood, the beauty and texture of river cobbles added distinction to a

With its stucco walls, square-lined massing, and flat roof, the Pine Apartments **(site 43)** reflect the elements of Art Moderne style. SHPO

few homes in town. One of the most graceful examples is a 1901 Queen Anne–style house **(site 37)** to which Frank Meinhart (the second owner) added a rich stone veneer. The house is unusual for its combination of cobble work and Queen Anne style and for its intricate use of small cobbles.

Native stone gave structure to a few houses as well. In 1907 Sherman Gill, a local builder, built a variation on the four-square theme for his own house **(site 7)**. Scrolled bracketing and a front bay window enliven his folk Victorian design, but it is the rugged blue-gray Corvallis stone that truly sets Gill's home apart.

During the Craftsman era, pre-formed concrete blocks with a stone look also gained popularity, and "cast stone" began to appear on many homes and business buildings. There are many such houses up the road in Stevensville where cast stone

When Frank Meinhart and his wife layered small river cobbles on the outside of this Queen Anne home **(site 37)**, they added a richness and texture more commonly seen in Craftsman-era buildings. SHPO

The deep blue-gray of native Corvallis stone lends a rugged strength to Sherman Gill's 1907 residence **(site 7)**. Such homes were uncommon in Hamilton, where lumber milling made wood houses the norm. SHPO

"Cast stone" was a form of concrete block that became a highly popular construction material during the early 1900s. Henry Grover's 1909 cast stone home **(site 36)** is a lively, eclectic design with its Queen Anne square tower, Classical columns, and Romanesque-arched window. SHPO

was locally manufactured, but in Hamilton, Henry Grover's house built in 1909 **(site 36)** is one of the very few buildings that used this technology. The blocks for this home were manufactured at the Stevensville concrete works.

Probably the most unusual home in Hamilton is the octagonal house of Other C. Wamsley **(site 10)**. A carpenter and farmer from Indiana, Wamsley had both "architectural training and an imaginative mind." For its ability to contain more space than a standard home, he chose an octagonal plan, and the construction of his "round house" in 1909 became the talk of the town. During the teens Wamsley, an excellent builder and craftsman, built many homes in Hamilton.

Promoted in 1849 by Orson S. Fowler with his publication *The Octagon House, A Home for All*, octagonal houses were rarities across the country. Other C. Wamsley, a local carpenter, built this one **(site 10)** for his family in 1909 and trimmed it with Shingle detailing and an eccentric square bay window on the second floor. SHPO

PUBLIC BUILDINGS

Across Montana and the West, public buildings often eloquently expressed the hopes of the residents of emerging towns. These buildings reached skyward, providing a stately presence and a lofty counterpoint to the business blocks and homes of the everyday world.

Like many courthouses constructed in Montana, the Ravalli County Courthouse **(site 31)**, built in 1900, was designed to reflect early-twentieth-century sentiment. During the first two decades of the 1900s, as farmers rushed into rural Montana, the number of counties swelled to fifty-six, and each new county required a courthouse. Resonating with the rhythms of ancient Greece and Rome, even the most modest of these buildings exudes an air of permanence, tradition, and grandeur.

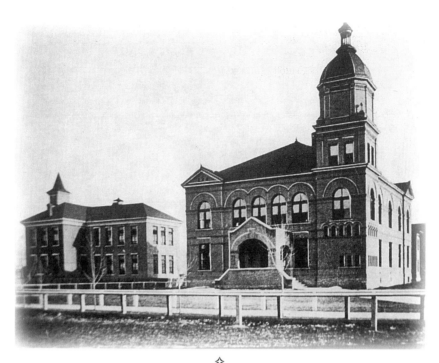

"To build or not to build a courthouse seems to be the issue," observed the Ravalli County *Democrat* in January 1900, just before the county launched one of its biggest building projects ever, an imposing brick Romanesque courthouse **(site 31)** designed by Missoula architect A. J. Gibson. BVHS

Just around the corner from the Ravalli County Courthouse is the Hamilton City Hall and Fire Station **(site 23)**. Designed by courthouse architect A. J. Gibson in 1906, the City Hall is a beautiful brick structure; its blocky symmetry and Romanesque arch detailing echo the courthouse design and reverberate across the Bitterroot, on buildings ranging from banks to schools to Daly's Tammany Castle **(site 4)**.

In budding western towns, schoolhouses were also symbols of community. Hamilton's first schools were wood frame buildings, followed in short order by three larger and more up-to-date brick schools. Yet even these sturdy buildings— Center School, old Washington School, and Jefferson School—

Hamilton's City Hall and Fire House (site 23), also designed by A. J. Gibson, echoes his design for the courthouse with its Romanesque arches and dominant square tower. BVHS

gave way to time and other town needs; the only historic school remaining today is the original 1929 portion of Hamilton High School (site 26), designed by Missoula architect H. E. Kirkemo.

Hand in hand with schools to educate the younger generation came libraries to provide for the edification of the entire community. During the late nineteenth century, Andrew Carnegie, famed industrialist from the steel mills in Pittsburgh, developed a plan for, as he put it, "improving the masses of the people" by providing them access to books and learning. Due to Carnegie's philanthropy, over sixteen hundred libraries were built across the nation between 1886 and 1917. Hamilton was one of seventeen towns in Montana to receive

Hamilton High School **(site 26)**, the last remaining historic school in town, reflects Colonial Revival design. BVHS

The Ravalli Public Library **(site 22)** captures the look of Carnegie libraries across the nation with its rectangular symmetry, temple-front central entrance, Classical pediment, and scrolled ornamentation. BVHS

a Carnegie Library, and the building (site 22) was completed in 1916.

Catering to residents' spiritual needs, several religious congregations built churches in Hamilton. Early on, services and Sunday schools were held in makeshift spaces—people's homes and unused space in store buildings and meeting halls. The Presbyterians built Hamilton's first church (site 30) in 1893. The Catholics soon followed, with the Irish-Catholic Marcus Daly helping to finance the building. A stunning Shingle-style church, St. Francis Catholic Church (site 33) was designed by A. F. Heide of Everett, Washington, and completed in 1896. Though Shingle

This historic view of Hamilton's churches displays the many beautiful variations of ecclesiastical architecture seen in the young community. Beginning at the lower right, and proceeding clockwise, they are Hamilton's Presbyterian Church (site 30); St. Paul's Episcopal Church (site 38); Methodist Episcopal Church North (site 9); First Christian Church (site 39); Methodist Episcopal Church South (formerly at Madison and Third, it is no longer standing); and at center, St. Francis Catholic Church (site 33). MHS Library

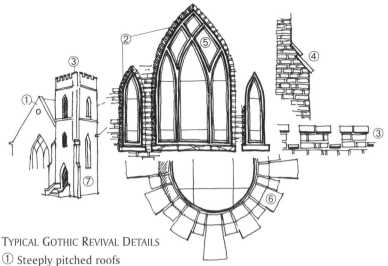

TYPICAL GOTHIC REVIVAL DETAILS

① Steeply pitched roofs
② Pointed arches and openings
③ Battlements (used for defense in medieval times)
④ Buttresses (supports projecting from the exterior of the building)
⑤ Tracery (decorative patterns within windows)
⑥ Wheel windows
⑦ Towers

was an unusual style choice for a church, Heide wrote in 1895, "the construction will be very simple and inexpensive" and rightly predicted that the building "will be a beauty."

Margaret Daly, on the other hand, was an Episcopalian and pledged to "donate liberally" to the building of that denomination's church. Designed by Reverend George Stewart of Missoula, St. Paul's Episcopal Church was completed in Gothic style in 1893 (site 38). In 1895 Marcus Daly reportedly offered town lots to encourage the building of other churches. Two Gothic-style churches soon followed. Daly's carpenters built the First Christian Church in 1895 (site 39) and the Methodist Episcopal Church North the following year (site 9).

One of the Daly family's most lasting contributions to Hamilton came after the death of Marcus Daly. When Daly's wife, Margaret, and children were planning a "suitable

Designed by H. E. Kirkemo, the Colonial-style Marcus Daly Memorial Hospital **(site 28)** was completed in 1931. In November that year *Pacific* *Builder and Engineer* magazine described the building as "a compromise between utility and beauty." BVHS

memorial" to Hamilton's town patriarch, they settled upon a community hospital. The Marcus Daly Memorial Hospital **(site 28)**, designed by H. E. Kirkemo, was completed in 1931. At the dedication Mrs. Daly's son-in-law concluded, "As the best possible memorial to the memory of her dear husband, Mrs. Margaret Daly presents to the people of the Bitter Root this fully equipped hospital, together with a sum of money to help maintain it. And she makes it the only condition, that this hospital shall always be free to those of all races, nationalities and to all creeds, and that politics shall never interfere in its management. Long may this hospital administer to the inhabitants of this happy valley."

Undoubtedly the largest public construction project in Hamilton's history was the building of the Rocky Mountain Laboratory in 1928 **(site 45,** see photograph page 25). Specially designed to contain the disease, the building had restricted labs, controlled access, rounded interior corners for easy cleansing, and special flannel flagging outside to facilitate detection of escaped ticks. Urgent need for the spotted fever vaccine spurred lab expansion. Housing a million and more ticks for vaccine production demanded space for the bugs and for their hosts—as many as six thousand rabbits and thirty thousand guinea pigs. With funds from depression-era public works programs, nine new buildings were added: three labs, two houses, and various support buildings.

RAILROAD AND INDUSTRY

Though birthed by the Anaconda Company and nurtured by the Missoula & Bitter Root Railroad, over time Hamilton has sadly lost many of her industrial buildings. Once the pulse of the town, the railroad depot that stood at the head of Main Street is gone. Nothing except a remnant of the dam remains of the Big Mill. Daly's granary and flour mill are gone and so is the rail stop at River Siding. Little remains of the brickyard where Patrick Cone "burned" bricks or of the Wanderer brickyard. Farm co-op sheds, where apple boomers once shipped out the fruits of their orchards, have all but disappeared.

Those industrial sites that do remain are important, if overlooked, pieces of Hamilton history. The Bitter Root Development Company Warehouse (site 21), with its metal coat of corrugated gray siding, appears nondescript yet reflects the importance of this company to the existence of the town. From spectator boxes on the upper floor, track fans watched horses on Daly's racetrack (once laid out where the athletic field is now).

Straight north along the tracks lies the warehouse zone from Hamilton's earliest years (site 20). The center of wholesale

Hamilton's Missoula & Bitter Root Valley Railroad Depot once stood at the head of Main Street, where it connected the community and the Big Mill to the outside world. MHS Photo Archives

The Ravalli Mills processed flour, grains, and cereals grown in the fertile Bitterroot Valley. No longer standing, it was located along the river on the north edge of town, near Adirondac Avenue. MHS Photo Archives

commerce during the railroad era, the fading red, wooden warehouses strung along the railroad line recall the days when milled flour, crop seeds, packed apples, lumber, and more awaited shipment on daily trains that ran the length of the valley.

Other industrial buildings still stand but are no longer in service—the Bozeman Cannery (site 8), which began packing the valley's apples, berries, and cherries in 1923; the Hamilton Feed Mill, which now houses a small collection of shops; an early cannery and granary off Marcus Street; a railroad shed at the foot of Main that is now a flower shop.

But still used to this day are the Ravalli County Fairgrounds (site 2) that in 1895 joined the twenty-two thousand acres of Daly's Bitter Root Stock Farm to the town of Hamilton. Year by year, for more than a century, the fairgrounds have chronicled each chapter in the unfolding story of Hamilton and the fruitful, beautiful Bitterroot Valley.

Hamilton's original symmetrical grid is evident in this aerial view of the town, taken in 1968 looking north. MHS Photo Archives

Hamilton Today

SINCE THE TIME of the Anaconda Company mill, the apple boomers, and the spotted fever pioneers, Hamilton has settled into a life of small-town comfort. Just far enough up the Bitterroot to remain serene and uncrowded, the town has kept its historic character. The downtown remains a healthy center of activity, serving the town and a large outlying region of rural homes and farms. Restaurants, shops, and other local businesses fill the historic downtown. The Rocky Mountain Laboratory is now a biotech research lab, still employing steady numbers of scientists.

The economy of the Bitterroot continues to revolve around agriculture and logging despite the devastating fires of summer 2000. Farming in the Bitterroot continues, dominated by dairies and poultry farms that sell to the nearby city of Missoula. Many old apple orchards still thrive alongside a new generation of fruit trees, while tree nurseries and organic truck farms do a brisk business.

In a twist on the traditional timbering of a hundred years ago, log home building has become big business in the Bitterroot. Log home companies offer Lincoln Log–style building kits, sales of which are not limited to the Rocky Mountain region or even North America. Among other exotic destinations, log kits from the valley have been shipped to England and Turkey.

Trading on the valley's exceptional beauty and mild climate, the town and surrounding area have attracted many out-of-state visitors in recent years who come to hunt, fish, and vacation in the Big Sky country. Some are smitten with the friendly, open life-style and settle in, building vacation and retirement homes from Lolo to Darby.

In the past decade, the descendants of Marcus and Margaret Daly sold most of the family's holdings, including the Bitter Root Stock Farm lands and buildings. The family mansion was acquired by the State of Montana, and it is now one of the state's finest museums. The Stock Farm fields are now a topflight golf course; adjacent property is being subdivided into housing tracts.

Preserving stories and artifacts from Hamilton's past, the Bitter Root Valley Historical Society now occupies the historic courthouse. With the help of the Daly Mansion and the historical society, stewards of the town's past ensure that the memories of Hamilton's first hundred years will endure and that the stories of earlier times will continue to be told.

Afterword

BY RUSS LAWRENCE

Charter member of the Daly Mansion Preservation Trust,
board member of the Downtown Hamilton Business Improvement District,
and owner of Chapter One Book Store

DOCUMENTING HAMILTON'S rich architectural history is useful and productive only if something is then done to ensure its preservation. This book is an important first step, as it cultivates an appreciation for the resources we now enjoy. We owe a debt of gratitude to the citizens of the last century for leaving us buildings that are functional, attractive, durable, and adaptable, as this book capably points out.

Hamilton's citizens today have two choices: making sure these buildings and resources are still in place a hundred years from now, while adding strong architectural statements of our own values, or continuing the trend in evidence along the Highway 93 "strip" of erecting utilitarian buildings with few aesthetic qualities that have a relatively short life expectancy.

A short-term view favors the second approach, which is related to the early "boom town" mentality mentioned in this book: slap up a building, open for business, and when the boom goes bust, quickly move on.

Hamilton deserves better than that, and several groups are now working to see that our past is preserved and that our future reflects a long-term outlook.

Those groups include the obvious—the Daly Mansion Preservation Trust and the Bitter Root Valley Historical Society, groups whose mission is explicitly related to upholding historical values—and the not so obvious. The Downtown Hamilton Business Improvement District (DHBID), created in 1998, recognized early that preserving the historical character of Hamilton's downtown would add to the value of the entire district.

The DHBID has approved guidelines that suggest remodeling efforts preserve the historical character of each building, without striving to conform to some fanciful "theme." New construction is encouraged to blend with the old, without trying to imitate it. This should result in a business district that offers variety in style with a unity of purpose.

The sense of nostalgia that a historic downtown business district evokes isn't entirely a wistful longing for simpler times: it reflects the fact that a pedestrian-friendly, varied retail/professional environment *works*. The architecture of Hamilton's first fifty years is beautiful in part because of its functionality. Parking in one place and walking to a large number of businesses within a block or two of each other, all the while browsing attractive window displays and perhaps picking up a coffee or snack, is a model that appeals because it makes sense.

Contrast that with the Highway 93 strip, where huge parking lots separate boxy buildings. Walking from one to another is not only unappealing, it's hazardous. The few exceptions stand out—Farmers State Bank created a beautiful building that echoes Hamilton's heritage, and a few historical buildings, converted to commercial use, grace the highway's otherwise blighted passage through town.

If you have enjoyed reading about Hamilton's history as related through its architecture and construction, then I encourage you to support the historical preservation efforts of the community. That long-term view will ensure that a hundred years from now when a book similar to this one is published to document Hamilton's unique and splendid architectural heritage, it will be thicker, rather than thinner, than the one you now hold.

Hamilton Time Line

PRIOR TO 1800 Bitterroot Valley center of Salish homeland

SEPTEMBER 1805 Lewis and Clark travel through Bitterroot Valley

1808–12 North West Company, Hudson's Bay Company, and Pacific Fur Company establish fur trapping and trading posts in western Montana

FEBRUARY 1824 Alexander Ross of Hudson's Bay Company travels up Bitterroot Valley and camps at Ross' Hole

1831, 1835, 1837, 1839 Salish send delegations east to request missionaries

SEPTEMBER 1841 Father Pierre-Jean DeSmet and fellow Jesuits found St. Mary's Mission (near present-day Stevensville)

1842 Bitterroot Valley included within newly created Oregon Territory

1850 John Owen purchases St. Mary's property for $250, the first land transaction recorded in Montana

1853 General Isaac I. Stevens surveys route for railroad line; Washington Territory created

JULY 7, 1855 Stevens party and tribes meet at Council Grove and negotiate Hellgate Treaty

1860 Missoula County created within Washington Territory

1861–65 Civil War

MARCH 1863 Congress creates Idaho Territory

1863 Thomas W. Harris takes "two wagons of vegetables, 10 plus beef cattle" from the Bitterroot to Virginia City and Bannack mining camps

1864 Montana Territory created

NOVEMBER 1871 U.S. government forces the Salish to move from the Bitterroot Valley to the Jocko Valley (today's Flathead Reservation)

1877 Fort Missoula constructed in response to demands by white settlers for military protection; flight of the Nez Perce through the Bitterroot Valley

1883 Northern Pacific Railroad builds through Montana

1886 Agent for Marcus Daly purchases ranch that becomes Bitter Root Stock Farm

1887–88 Construction of Missoula & Bitter Root Valley Railroad

1890 Town of Hamilton founded

1891 Large-scale timber harvest begins

1892 Bitterroot National Forest established

1893 Ravalli County created from Missoula County; Stevensville named county seat

1894 U.S. Government Land Office cites Daly's Bitter Root Development Company for illegally cutting timber on public land

NOVEMBER 1898 County seat moves to Hamilton

1900 Marcus Daly dies; Hamilton population 1,257

1905 Dinsmore Irrigation and Development Company incorporates; apple boom begins

1909 Bitterroot Inn and Charlos Heights Clubhouse, designed by internationally acclaimed architect Frank Lloyd Wright, built

1910 Hamilton population over 3,000

1914–19 World War I (U.S. enters war in 1917)

1920 Canyon Creek Schoolhouse converted to Rocky Mountain spotted fever research lab

1928 Rocky Mountain Laboratory completed

1929 Great Depression begins

1930s U.S. government constructs nine new buildings at Rocky Mountain Laboratory

1939–45 World War II (U.S. enters 1941); Rocky Mountain Laboratory manufactures vaccines as part of the war effort

1941 Margaret Daly dies

1987 Daly Mansion acquired by the State of Montana

Suggested Reading

Much of the information for this book came from the community resource survey conducted in 1987–88, under the auspices of the State Historic Preservation Office of Montana.

Kirk Michels and the Hamilton Historic Resource Survey team summarized the results of their community survey in "Hamilton's Historic Buildings: 1890–1940," offprints of which can be purchased at the Bitter Root Valley Historical Society. A full record of the community survey is housed in the Montana State Historic Preservation Office, P.O. Box 201202, Helena, MT 59620-1202, as is Patricia Bik's National Register nomination for the Rocky Mountain Laboratory. Copies of inventories or the nomination may be obtained by writing, or by calling (406) 444-7715.

OTHER VALUABLE RESOURCES INCLUDE THE FOLLOWING:

Bitter Root Valley Historical Society. *Bitterroot Trails: Volumes 1–3.* Hamilton: privately published, 1982, 1998.

Grant, Henry H. *This is My Bitterroot.* Hamilton: privately published, 1997.

Harden, Victoria Angela. *Rocky Mountain Spotted Fever: History of a Twentieth-Century Disease.* Baltimore: Johns Hopkins University Press, 1990.

Johnson, Donald L. "Frank Lloyd Wright's Architectural Projects in the Bitterroot Valley, Montana, 1909–1910." *Montana The Magazine of Western History* 37 (Summer 1987): 12-25.

Langton, Jeffrey H. *The Victor Story: History of a Bitter Root Valley Town.* Missoula: Pictorial Histories Publishing Co., 1985.

Lawrence, Russ. *Montana's Bitterroot Valley: Just Short of Paradise.* Stevensville, Mont.: Stoneydale Press, 1999.

Powell, Ada. *The Dalys of the Bitterroot.* Hamilton: privately published, 1979.

———. *Copper Green and Silver.* Hamilton: privately published, 1993.

Powell, Ada, and Carolyn Jones. *Hello Hamilton.* Hamilton: privately published, 1988.

Stevensville Historical Society. *Montana Genesis.* Missoula: Mountain Press Publishing Co., 1971.

Index of Building Sites